A
Workshop
—on—

Time
Management

A Workshop on

Time Management

Ann Roecker

Lamplighter Books Grand Rapids,
Michigan
Zondervan Publishing House

A Workshop on Time Management
Copyright © 1988 by Ann Roecker

Lamplighter Books are published by the Zondervan Publishing House
1415 Lake Drive, S.E., Grand Rapids, Michigan 49506

Library of Congress Cataloging-in-Publication Data

Roecker, Ann.
　A workshop on time management / by Ann Roecker.
　　p. cm.
　"Lamplighter books."
　Includes bibliographical references.
　ISBN 0-310-37931-8
　1. Women—Time management. 2. Time—Biblical teaching. I. Title.
HQ1221.R67　　1988
640'.43'024042—dc19　　　　　　　　　　　　　　　　88–17400
　　　　　　　　　　　　　　　　　　　　　　　　　　　　CIP

Edited by John Sloan, Mary McCormick

Printed in the United States of America

88　89　90　91　92　93 / DP / 10　9　8　7　6　5　4　3　2　1

CONTENTS

INTRODUCTION

The number of seminars and books currently available on time management are legion. In various and sundry ways, they teach us to establish our priorities, plan our schedules in writing, delegate the disagreeable, and say "no" without guilt—all of this with the subtle assumption that our lives are always overcrowded with interesting people, our talents constantly in demand, and our phones forever ringing with yet another compelling opportunity.

Though such an assumption, intended or not, is far from reality for those of us who are not Lee Iacocca or Jane Fonda, it is little wonder that we flock to the bookstores to learn how to better manage our time. In a day when 48.5 million women are in the work force,[1] the pressures on our existence have increased considerably. We must now dress for success, be upwardly mobile, get an MBA, invest in stock, know

[1] *Statistical Abstracts of the United States—1985*, U.S. Department of Commerce Bureau of Census.

how to use a computer, speed read a book every few days, and travel for professional purposes with satisfactory regularity—and of course we must go to an aerobics class at least three times a week, with an occasional marathon thrown in. It is a noisy, unforgiving world.

It is no different for the woman who works at home.[2] She no longer "raises" her children; now she must "cultivate" them, a process whereby she rocks junior to sleep to the tunes of Beethoven and Rachmaninoff, teaches him to swim at six weeks, and coaches him to say "Daddy" in English, French, and Chinese—all of this to prime him for Harvard, and eventually, the Presidency. Of course today's housewife has other duties besides shaping kids who think like Einstein and look like the Brady Bunch. She also must hold a city council seat, write a bestselling novel and keep her husband deliriously happy.

As exaggerated as these portraits may be (or are they?), the point remains: many real and imagined demands are made on our time and somehow we must manage it. The fact is, we *want* to manage it. We want our time, and thus our lives, to be significant; we want them to be satisfying; and if at all possible, we want them to be sane.

Fortunately, we have someone to show us the way—Jesus Christ. As a man He was never frenzied, never anxious, never unorganized, never out of control—and He *never* succumbed to the superficial and burdensome tenets of His culture. In an extraordinary way, He lived graciously, profoundly and unfettered in the time and space He Himself invented. He beckons us to do the same.

---

[2] According to economist Ruth Leger Sivard, the labor value of housewives is $4 trillion per year; *Time*, August 5, 1985, p. 39.

Part I

GETTING PERSPECTIVE

1

WHO'S GOT TIME?

Everyone who is seriously involved in the pursuit of science becomes convinced that a spirit is manifest in the laws of the universe—a spirit vastly superior to that of man, and one in the face of which we with our modest powers must feel humble.

Albert Einstein

In 1905, a 26-year-old German-born physicist named Albert Einstein ventured beyond the normal definitions of the universe to suggest that time is relative; that the faster one travels, the slower time is. In practical terms, this means that if you were on a spaceship traveling near the speed of light,[1] you would reach the center of the galaxy in a mere 21 years,[2]

---

[1] The speed of light is 186,000 miles per second. At that speed, light can circumvent the Earth seven times per second.

[2] The center of our galaxy, the Milky Way, is 30,000 light years, or 176,340,000,000,000,000 miles away.

according to clocks aboard the spaceship. During those 21 years of travel time, however, 30,000 years will have passed on Earth where speed is slower, and thus time is faster. All of this because time is relative.[3] If you find this at once inspiring and incomprehensible, you certainly are not alone; it is an established fact that Albert Einstein forever altered the foundations of science and our understanding of the cosmos.

As brilliant and startling as Einstein's conclusions are, Christians for centuries have known in more general terms that time is not eternal, that time is not unchanging, that time is not the absolute ruler of our lives. Only God is eternal and unchanging. Only God is the ruler of all that exists. Time is His creation, it is under His control. It is His; He owns it; and for His own purposes, He has given each one of us a small but remarkable piece of it, and we must therefore discover what He wants us to do with it.

1. Who is God, according to the following verses? Read and summarize in your own words.

>   *Genesis 1:1*   *Colossians 1:16–17*
>   *John 1:3*   *Revelation 4:11*

_____

_____

2. Summarize what these verses say about God's commitment to His creation.

>   *Deuteronomy 31:6*   *Matthew 10:29–31*
>   *Isaiah 40:26*   *John 3:16*

_____

_____

---

[3] Sagan, Carl, *Cosmos*, (New York: Random House, 1980), 206–7.

3. What is God like—the God who created time and still is ruler over it—according to these verses? Read and summarize.

1 John 4:16   *Psalm 116:5*
1 Corinthians 1:9   *Psalm 147:5*
1 Timothy 1:17

_____

_____

I am willing to predict that because of space travel, by the end of the century, our churches will be full again.

Ray Bradbury

4. History tells us that God invaded time on Earth through His son, Jesus Christ. We do not know if He has invaded time on the other planets He has created, but we do know He has invaded time on ours. At the beginning of His public ministry, Christ summarized how He planned to use His time during the final three years He was here. Read Luke 4:16–21 and list the things Christ intended to do. From what you know of Christ's life, did He accomplish these objectives? ___

_____

_____

5. The following verses suggest the basis on which Christ determined how He used His time. Read and summarize.

John 4:34   *Matthew 14:23*
John 5:19

_____

_____

_____

6. Was Jesus ever tempted to make plans apart from the sovereign design of the Father, according to Matthew 4:3–10? _____

_____

_____

7. Was Jesus ever uncomfortable with the demands His Father made on His life, according to Matthew 26:36–39? __

_____

_____

> *If you want a religion to make you feel comfortable, I certainly don't recommend Christianity.*
>
> C.S. Lewis

8. Despite His desire to forego the cross in the Garden of Gesthemane, what did Jesus do, according to Philippians 2:8? _____

_____

9. What was the result of Jesus' surrender to His Father's will, according to Philippians 2:9–11? _____

_____

_____

_____

10. God gives many promises to His people as they give their time and their lives over to Him. Briefly summarize in your own words those listed here.

Proverbs 3:6	*Mark 10:29–30*
Isaiah 40:30–31	*Luke 12:11–12*
Matthew 6:30–33	*John 14:1–3*

_____

_____

> *I have held many things in my hands, and I have lost them all; but whatever I have placed in God's hands, that I still possess.*
>
> Martin Luther

11. Read Matthew 6:33 and discuss what you think it means to seek God first in the use of our time. _____

_____

_____

12. Based on your own experience, discuss why we often hesitate to abandon our time to the Lord. _____

_____

_____

13. What enables us to seek His plans on the use of our time according to Hebrews 11:1–2? _____

_____

_____

14. Read Hebrews 10:22–23, and list the things that cultivate our faith. _____

_____

_____

15. Conclude by reading Psalm 19.

TIME OUT
By Carol Kuykendall

Carol Kuykendall, the author of *Learning To Let Go*, is a freelance writer. She also has frequent speaking engagements, is active in numerous volunteer endeavors and has appeared on *The Today Show* with her sister, *Knot's Landing* star Joan Van Ark. Carol deftly balances her active professional life with an equally active personal life that includes her husband, Lynn Kuykendall, an attorney, and their three children. Her advice on managing time . . .

As a writer who works at home, I have some unique challenges in terms of managing my time. The first challenge is setting up in my home a work space that is functional and efficient. I invested in some supplies, such as stand-up files, paperclips, tape dispensers, and a giant coffee mug for sharpened pencils, pens and markers. (To be organized, it's important to have your tools at your fingertips.)

But the single most time-saving device surprised me. It seemed small at first, but it has made a large difference. It is a Rolodex. I'm amazed how efficiently I can find numbers and information I used to search for in phone or address books. I keep businesses, friends, professional contacts, babysitters—everyone I need—listed on this Rolodex. I even have my credit card numbers and the social security numbers of family members on it.

A second challenge is protecting my work time, especially difficult because I work at home. I have learned to say "no" more often and to set aside the hours between 8:30 a.m. and 3:00 p.m. for work. I try to say "yes" to the activities or distractions that are important, however, even if they are not on my "to do" list. To discern the "yes" answers, I ask myself, "Will this make a difference in five years?"

2

A TIME FOR EVERYTHING

*Great men never complain about the lack of time.
Alexander the Great and John Wesley accomplished
everything they did in twenty-four-hour days.*

Fred Smith

"I don't have time."

We've all said it at one time or another with varying degrees of complacency, frustration, or panic. Translated into more specific terms, it means, "I don't want to take the time." More often it means, "My life feels overcrowded with an unmanageable host of demands on my energies."

Whether we do not want to take the time—or cannot—we must understand that we do, in fact, have time. We have enough time for everything God wants us to do. Ecclesiastes 3:1 (NASB) states, "There is an appointed time for everything. And there is a time for every event under heaven." Never once does God in His Word suggest that He requires us to do something that He does not provide for us the time in which to do it. Nor does He intimate that we must hurry and worry to overload our schedules to the brink of insanity and frustration to please Him.

Certainly there are times when we can legitimately say, "I don't have time," and mean, "I do not feel that God wants me to invest my time in that way right now." But still, if we are honest with ourselves we have to admit that there are occasions when we don't accomplish everything we want to or think we ought to. It is on those occasions that we must ask ourselves if we are living by God's agenda—or our own.

Let's examine Jesus' life and see how He "had time for everything."

1. Read Luke 10:38–42 and note what Jesus said to Martha who, we can postulate, was feeling a lack of time and/or resources to complete the task at hand.

_____

_____

2. Undoubtedly, Martha expected Jesus to respond more sympathetically to her situation. Why do you think Jesus responded to Martha in the way He did? What did He want her to understand? _____

_____

_____

Work is not always required of a man. There is such a thing as sacred idleness, the cultivation of which is now fearfully neglected.

George MacDonald

3. Martha probably was a conscientious, diligent individual. Look up the word "diligent" in the dictionary; then read

Proverbs 13:4. What is the difference between Martha's approach to her circumstances and being diligent? _____

_____

_____

4. Read Matthew 17:24–27 and Luke 9:12–17. Note how Jesus provided more than adequately the time and resources for His disciples to fulfill the tasks that He—and others—required of them. _____

_____

_____

> My brother Charles, amid the difficulties of our early ministry, used to say, "If the Lord would give me wings, I would fly." I used to say, "If the Lord bade me fly, I would trust Him for the wings."
>
> John Wesley

5. Read the following verses and identify the kind of activity in which the disciples were engaged. Note how Jesus scheduled for His disciples a wide variety of experiences, and "a time for everything."

> *Luke 5:4–7*   *Luke 11:1–4*
> *Luke 6:1*   *Matthew 17:1–5*
> *Luke 10:1–3*   *John 13:5*

_____

_____

6. The way God would have us use our time often is not the same way He would have others use their time. Read John 21:20–22 and summarize what Jesus said when Peter tried to compare the plans the Lord had for him with the plans He had for "the disciple whom Jesus loved." (Many scholars identify this disciple as being John, who was a close colleague of Peter throughout most of his life. Tradition tells us that the Lord's plans for Peter and John were, in fact, quite different. Peter died publicly, crucified hanging upside down; John died quietly in exile on the Greek island of Patmos.)

7. In what areas are you vulnerable to comparison? How does this affect the way you determine the use of your time?

_____

_____

8. Think of a situation in your own life when you felt you didn't have enough time or resources to accomplish what you felt was necessary. Can you see a difference between what you wanted to get done (or someone else wanted you to get done) and perhaps what God wanted from you? _____

_____

_____

9. Make a list of all the things in the past few weeks for which you have not "had time." Next to each item, identify why you were not able to get it done. You might want to evaluate whether God is actually leading you to do it, if there is a lesson to be learned in not being able to do it, or if a different approach to the task is in order. _____

_____

_____

10. Conclude by reading Ecclesiastes 3:1−8.

We never shall have any more time. We have, and have always had, all the time there is.

Arnold Bennett

TIME OUT
By Katharine Raybin

Kathy Raybin is co-founder/director of the Women's Ministries at First Presbyterian Church in Boulder, Colorado, and is locally famous for the time she devotes to numerous volunteer endeavors and to the needs of others. She and her husband Jim, a psychiatrist, have two children. About managing time, she says . . .

My "in-box" was newly filled each morning with work to be done at my first job after college graduation. Each day the supervisor of the department would put into the box correspondence for me to answer by sales letters promoting our textbooks. I did the routine and simple ones first, letting the more complex problems sink to the bottom of the pile. As new letters were added daily, the bottom of the pile got farther and farther down. Some day, I thought, I'll do those hard ones. But I noticed that no matter how many other letters I wrote, the hard ones didn't disappear. Finally, I *had* to answer the tough letters.

The "lesson of the in-box" helps me today, 20 years later, with time management in my daily life. The tough jobs do not disappear by ignoring them, or by saving them for some other time, or by wishing someone else would do them. In fact, the easy tasks don't disappear either, until I *do* them. So, although my techniques vary for handling the tasks of my days, I'm aware that the time the Lord gives me for each day must be applied to the jobs of that day.

One of my favorite techniques in handling my daily tasks is to do parts of larger tasks in small pieces of available time instead of waiting for the big chunk of time that never seems to come. This is part of my "little-tiny-baby-steps" trick that applies to climbing a mountain or running a long distance. By doing little bits at a time, the undone part of a project becomes more and more manageable.

Another helpful technique I've found is to schedule my time backwards from when the job needs to be done, figuring time allotments for different fragments of the task.

Finally, I'm coming to understand that open spaces of time are to be managed too—they're for looking and listening and learning and realizing. They, too, are precious gifts from the Lord.

3

THE TIME WARP

Mistakes are just another way of doing things.

Author Unknown

On a recent business trip to New York City, I found myself with an extra half hour between meetings. My previous meeting had been on 6th Avenue; reason told me that 7th Avenue, the address of my next meeting, was not far away. Since I had the time and being that it was an exceptionally pleasant fall afternoon, I decided to walk to it rather than take a cab.

Optimistically I made a beeline for 7th Avenue, but soon found myself in the middle of the red-light district, a scenic section of the city that is characterized by loitering women, "adult" bookstores and X-rated movie theaters. I was unable to spot a street address, but quickly surmised that I was at the *wrong* end of 7th Avenue—if I was on 7th Avenue at all—for certain, I did not want to be at the location I had reached.

Time for Plan B: I hailed a cab. But it seemed as if the cab drivers didn't want to be in the red-light district either. Every approaching yellow car passed me by, until finally, a frustrating 25 minutes later, one cab slowed down and I jumped in before he could raise a protest.

"Yeah, lady, you're at the wrong end of the city, all right," the driver affirmed when I gave him the address of my destination.

Needless to say, I was late for my appointment, made worse by the fact that I was meeting with a large, well-monied corporate foundation to solicit funds on behalf of one of my clients. Dashing in late, disheveled, and disoriented was not my idea of making a good impression. I should have confirmed the location of my 7th Avenue meeting before attempting to walk to it, but I did not. Alas, I had mismanaged my time.

Time is like that; it is easily mismanaged. We can make heroic attempts at managing it perfectly, but perfection is hard to come by in an imperfect world overpopulated with imperfect people. Therefore, if we want to learn to manage our time effectively, we also must learn to manage it realistically; we must cultivate the skills that enable us to maximize our inevitable failures.

I would like to consider three of those skills:
1) The ability to change course
2) The ability to recover quickly
3) The ability to forgive oneself and others repeatedly

SKILL I: THE ABILITY TO CHANGE COURSE

Those who cannot change their minds, cannot change anything.

George Bernard Shaw

1. Read Acts 16:6–10, which describes a portion of Paul's second missionary journey. Note in this passage that Paul had planned to go to Bithynia, but was not able to make the journey. *And so he changed his plans* and went to a different city.

2. What kept Paul from living out his original plans? _____

_____

_____

3. What do you think enabled Paul to adjust readily to new plans? _____

_____

_____

4. What do you think would have happened if Paul had not changed course? _____

_____

_____

5. What attitudes would have kept him from changing his plans, despite the obvious leading of the Spirit? _____

_____

_____

6. What are some feelings you experience when you plan one thing, and for whatever reasons, you are not able to live them out? _____

_____

_____

7. Read Proverbs 22:3 and summarize what this passage says about flexibility. _____

By the way, after explaining my saga to the people with whom I was meeting in New York, they merely laughed, saying, "That's New York for you!" We went on to have an enjoyable and productive encounter, despite my poor time management. I appreciated their flexibility.

SKILL II: THE ABILITY TO RECOVER QUICKLY

Whenever I make a bum decision, I just go out and make another one.

Harry Truman

If anyone was a victim of the roller-coaster syndrome, it was Joseph, one of the Old Testament's most compelling heroes. The ups and downs that characterized his life would have left most of us dizzy and disillusioned. A brief summary of the consecutive events in Joseph's life reads something like this:

(Up) Finds favor with Israel, his father. (Gen. 37:3)

(Down) Sold into Egyptian slavery by jealous brothers. (Gen. 37:18–36)

(Up) Finds favor with Potiphar, the captain of Pharaoh's guard. Potiphar puts Joseph in charge of his household. (Gen. 39:1–6)

(Down) Potiphar's wife falsely accuses him of foul play. Joseph gets dismissed . . . goes to jail. (Gen. 39:7–20)

(Up) Finds favor with the chief jailer. He makes Joseph overseer of the other prisoners. (Gen. 39:19–21)

(Down) Joseph's imprisonment is prolonged by unfaithful friends. (Gen. 40)

(Up) Finds favor with Pharaoh, who places him in charge of his business affairs. His position in Pharaoh's court eventually enables him to save the brothers who sold him into slavery from starvation. (Gen. 41–45)

1. Given these wrenching highs and lows, it is probably safe to say that Joseph's PRR (personal recovery rate) was remarkable. Review the passages listed above and write down what seems to characterize each "up" and each "down" of Joseph's life. _____

_____

_____

2. Why do you think Joseph was able to recover so quickly? _____

_____

_____

3. What personal skills and qualities of character do you think enabled Joseph to make each "down" an "up"? _____

_____

_____

4. How does the possession of these qualities of character affect time management? _____

_____

_____

5. How does the lack of them affect time management? ___

_____

_____

SKILL III: THE ABILITY TO FORGIVE YOURSELF AND OTHERS REPEATEDLY

I mean can you fall and get up again without crying and mount again and fall again and yet not be afraid of falling.

C.S. Lewis in *The Horse & His Boy*

1. How often did Christ tell us to forgive someone who sins against us (Matt. 18:21−22)? _____

_____

_____

2. Near the end of Christ's life, Peter, one of His closest friends on Earth, failed to support Him in His most difficult hour. Later, Peter publicly denied any association with Him. Read John 21:12−19 and note how Jesus quickly forgave Peter, pushing His feckless friend on to new heights of discipleship.

3. How do you think it would have affected the progress of the early church and Peter's involvement in it, if Jesus had not forgiven him? _____

_____

_____

4. Ask the Lord to show you if there is anyone you have not forgiven; also ask Him to help you actively forgive anyone He brings to mind. Conclude by reading 1 John 1:9 and Psalm 103:10−13.

TIME OUT
By Gwen Brown

As Program Assistant of First Presbyterian Church in Boulder, Colorado, Gwen Brown is interrupted on the average of 15 times per minute. "Ask Gwen," "Gwen will know," Gwen is in charge of that one," are common reverberations in this active, 2,000-member congregation. The truth is, Gwen *does* know. She is disgustingly well organized, and despite her story below, I have never known her to let anything fall through the cracks. She has, however, saved the necks of numerous individuals by bringing to their attention a missed item, a forgotten step, a blatant oversight. She is a network unto herself . . . and of time management, she says . . .

I love calendars and enjoy projects with many details. I picture myself doing a juggling act—keeping four bosses and numerous committees reasonably happy, my home reasonably in order, and my marriage reasonably on track. Indeed, a not-so-small measure of pride comes in. But then one or more of the "jugglees" tumbles out of place. Just recently I remembered to order 2,100 sheets of custom-cut paper for a bulletin *two* days before it was to be printed. I'm thankful that I don't depend on my efficiency alone, but rather on a strong network of relationships. Knowing that the service rep at the paper company was my co-worker's personal friend enabled me to get special handling and the bulletins printed on time. I had dropped the ball, despite the fact that the bulletin paper had been on several "to do" lists. But my network picked up my fumble and ran for the touchdown.

Having a network on whom to call is another way of saying "It's not *what* you know, but *whom* you know" in a positive way. Earlier in my career I often found the bureaucratic maze of a large university frustrating and time—consuming. I learned to save time by going to the person who actually processed the form or made the final decision. But more importantly, as I connected the task with a real person, I realized the relational dimension in every job.

Relational networks speak of interdependence. We are not intended to go it alone, even in the area of time management. We are much more effective as a team than as lone rangers. "Body life" as pictured in 1 Corinthians 12 certainly is needed in our everyday tasks. And so relational networks temper my pride of personal efficiency, enhance my ability to juggle successfully, and encourage me to respond cheerfully when I get yet another caller saying, "Gwen, I need you to . . ."

Part II

MAKING PLANS

4

BUILDING DREAMS

Whenever anything is being accomplished it is being done, I have learned, by a monomaniac with a mission.

Peter Drucker

I have long been fascinated by the life of Christopher Columbus. A remarkable 15th-century man, he was driven by an unshakable conviction that he could reach the east by sailing west, thus proving that the Earth is round. History tells us that it was not a popular notion. The church accused Columbus of heresy, the royal court accused him of arrogance, and most of Europe accused him of foolishness of the worst kind. Yet the west—and God—still beckoned; and Columbus went on to become one of western culture's most pivotal and inspiring figures.

What enabled Columbus to overcome adversity and discouragement, and to stand alone against his numerous critics? Evidence suggests that it was because he had a dream that was stronger than his difficulties, a dream that spoke more loudly to him than the choir of voices that opposed him. And evidence suggests that it was because he possessed a deeply rooted sense that God had a purpose for him on the open seas.

God also has a purpose for us. Each of us is asked and equipped to contribute something to history that no one else in quite the same way is equipped to contribute. Unless we understand our destiny, unless we understand why we are alive, it becomes most difficult to manage our time. We have no basis upon which to make a decision as to how to use our time, we have no resolve when adversity or pointless alternatives come our way, and we have no sense that managing our time effectively truly matters. But given what Scripture tells us, we must conclude that our lives do matter; that we do have a purpose; and that the world is intended to be a different place because of our presence on the planet, not only corporately as Christians, but amazingly, as individuals.

1. Read the following verses and summarize what they say about God's purpose for our lives.

Matthew 22:37–40	*2 Corinthians 5:20*
Matthew 28:18	*Ephesians 2:10*
John 10:10	*1 Thessalonians 4:7–8*
Romans 14:7–8	

Have a full life - Love him & neighbors
Have a abunte B life.

Destiny waits in the hand of God, not in the hands of statesmen.

T.S. Eliot

2. At times our purpose and our dreams can seem generalized and self-imposed. How can we know for certain that God has a specific purpose for us as individuals? Read 1 Corinthians 12:4–7 and summarize _____

Everyone has a gift & ministry

3. According to John 15:5, what must we do to fulfill the purpose God has for us? _____

Abiding in Christ

4. Read and summarize the following verses, noting that God promises to fulfill His own purpose for us.

     Isaiah 46:9–11   *Job 42:2*
     Psalm 48:14

What He promises He will do — He will our God's forever

5. To what degree can we rely on God to fulfill His purpose for us, according to these verses?

     Isaiah 49:15   *1 Corinthians 1:9*

God will never forget us —
God is faithful in all He does

6. Sometimes it is difficult for us to appreciate our uniqueness and our importance in God's scheme. How did Moses react when God revealed to him His purpose? (Exod. 3:11; 4:10) *He didn't think he could do it*

7. And Jeremiah (Jer. 1:5–6)? *He was to young and cauldn't do it.*

Few scuttlers (humans) are at home with their uniqueness.

> *Calvin Miller in The Valiant Papers*

8. Among the first items on Jesus' agenda for His disciples
was to help them understand the purpose He had for their
lives. What did He tell them with regard to their importance
and their destiny in the following verses?

Matthew 4:19   Matthew 5:13–16

9. Read Matthew 16:17–19, noting the Lord's purpose for
Peter. Did He fulfill the purpose He outlined for Peter,
according to Acts 3:1–7 and 4:13–20? *He was to be the foundation of the Church. Preached to the Jews (Performed miracles)*

God has cared to make me for Himself . . . and has
called me that which I like best.

> George MacDonald

10. In living out your own destiny, ask yourself—and
God—the following questions. Work through the questions,
taking several days to answer them if necessary.

a. Have there been times when you felt that God
indicated a "calling" for your life? What Scripture verse(s),
people, and circumstances did He use?

b. Are you positioning your life and using your time with this "calling" in mind?

c. Are you spending your time in ways that are keeping you from focusing on the unique contribution God wants you to make? If so, what do you need to do to adjust your schedule to better focus your time on God's specific purpose for you?

d. If you are unsure of your purpose and abilities, work through these questions:

What have you always dreamed of being/doing?
What needs do you see in the world around you
*   that you know you can meet?*
How do other people seem to benefit most
*   from you?*
What do you do that seems to tangibly further
*   God's work?*
Who are your role models? Why do you readily
*   identify with them?*

Spend time praying, asking God to show you His purpose for you and what work He wants you to accomplish.

Man forgets his purpose and thus he forgets who he is and what life means.

Francis Schaeffer

TIME OUT
By Karen Oliver

Karen Oliver has a master's degree in journalism from the University of Oregon, and although she is still trying to decide what to do "when she grows up," she has been a radio news reporter, script writer, advertising "voice," and editor, among her numerous journalistic pursuits. She is given to wild spurts of creative genius, and has done more to inspire the vision and affirm the purpose of this writer than any other living person. She is single and resides in Palo Alto, California. Of time management, she says . . .

My idea of time management used to be to get up in the morning and move as fast as I could for as long as I could. This, obviously, was not designed for efficiency or health. Now, if I have an abundance of things to accomplish (typical), I list any specific appointments and errands and their geographic location on a master list. This helps me schedule my errands around not just the time of appointments, but their location. That way I don't waste time running zigzag through my day.

I also believe that time management is space management. So that I don't waste time finding things, I have created a pile for everything and everything is in its pile. I live in too small a space to be able to have a *place* for everything, and since most of my "everything" is paper, it piles easily. Good furniture arrangement for "easy access" to those piles also helps, unfortunately, my current living situation means I have to redefine what I mean by 'easy access." Here, if I can get to it by running over my bed, it's easy access.

Believe it or not, I have a strong need for order, but I am not willing to drive myself to be excruciatingly neat. I have too little energy and too little time to spend trying to make myself into what I'm not. I find that I need to create an order that works for me, even if it makes a friend roll her eyes heavenward and pray for my (literal) deliverance from this pit.

5

ESTABLISHING PRIORITIES

There is no surprise more wonderful than the surprise of being loved; it is God's finger on man's shoulder.

Charles Morgan

His name was Ralph Patton, but no one called him that. His friends called him Pat; we called him Pop-op. A self-made man who had worked nights during the Depression to put himself through school, he ultimately landed a job as an artist for the *Chicago Daily News,* where he befriended the likes of Herb Block, the brilliant political cartoonist, and Chester Gould, the creator of the "Dick Tracy" comic strip. Strikingly handsome, he was a male model on the side.

Eventually he established his own advertising agency in the Chicago area where his intelligence, curiosity, energy, and warmth seemed to attract for him an endless stream of friends, not the least of which were his five grandchildren, among whom I was counted. A visit to Chicago always was a rare experience—he made sure that it was—and when we returned home to Colorado, it was not long before we found a letter from him waiting for us in the mail.

His were no ordinary letters. They were typed on textured art paper, over a water color he had drawn depicting the predictably humorous and lyrical contents of his epistle. If we had gone to the zoo during our visit, he would draw my brothers, sisters, and me hanging precariously from a fence throwing peanuts to the seals; if we had gone to the museum (and we almost always had), he would draw us skipping through the galleries making noisy, delightful nuisances of ourselves. Thus every letter from Pop-op was an original work of art. We treasured these postal gems, as did his numerous friends, all of whom received an equally generous expression of his affection for them.

I'll admit, it was a lot of work. A hurriedly scratched note probably would have sufficed. Still, it would not have been the same, and although he died 20 years ago, Pop-op's exuberance and creativity is forever etched in my imagination.

I would not be surprised to learn, however, that a number of items were frequently left undone on his list of things to do—because he always had plenty of time for loving other people. I have a feeling he knew something important about priorities.

1. According to Matthew 22:34–38, what is God's first priority for our lives? *We are to love Him*

2. What is His second priority according to Matthew 22:39–40? *Love our neighbor*

_____

_____

3. Discuss, or write in the space provided, what you imagine a relationship with Christ would be like if these were not His priorities? _____

_____

_____

> *Our Lord does not care so much for the importance of our works as for the love with which they are done.*
>
> Teresa of Avila

4. In the Gospel of John, Jesus refers to His "Father" nearly 100 times; in the Sermon on the Mount, He refers to "your Father" 14 times. What does this repeated emphasis on a relationship with the Father say about Jesus' priorities? _____

He loved his father. Wanted to do his will.

5. Read 1 Peter 5:7–9 and list two reasons Jesus wants us to root our priorities and affections in a relationship with the Father? *Doesn't want us to worry. He wants to carry our burdens if we will let him.*

6. Read Matthew 5:43–48 and note the scope Christ intends our love for others to have. To what degree do you think our "enemies" are a priority to the Lord? _____

_____

_____

7. Jesus spent a good part of His 3-year public ministry with people. Read the following verses and list the various ways He spent His time, noting the interest many different kinds of people had in Him.

Luke 4:40–42   Luke 7:11, 36
Luke 5:29–30   Luke 7:36
Luke 8:40   Luke 12:1
Luke 9:12–17, 37   Luke 14:25
Luke 9:37

*He worked with all kind of people —
large group — one on one — medium groups*

If a man has no time or only a short time for seeing people, you can be fairly sure that he is neither very important nor very busy.

John Spenser Churchill

8. In Luke 8:40–50, Jesus was on His way to raise from the dead the daughter of an important community leader. His journey was slowed by the crowds and interrupted by the needs of a woman who had been bleeding for 12 years. How did Jesus handle this imposition on His time? How would you have handled it? What does this episode say about Jesus' priorities? _____

_____

_____

9. Summarize what Jesus said in Matthew 8:21–22 to the man who was letting family obligations determine his priorities? Was Jesus saying our families shouldn't be important to us? If not, what was He saying? Then read Luke 18:28–30, noting what Jesus assured Peter. _____

_____

_____

10. In an attempt to determine your own priorities take one day this week and list everything you did that day. Don't worry about being too detailed; the details can tell you a lot. Then review your schedule and write down what your five top priorities were that day as reflected in the way you spent your time. How do your priorities compare with Christ's priorities—how are they the same; how are they different? List any adjustments you need to make. _____

_____

_____

11. What does Christ ask us to keep in mind as we adjust our priorities to match His in these verses?

> *Matthew 7:7–11*   *Isaiah 41:10*
> *John 14:16*

_____

_____

That's the problem with businessmen. They are forever planning to succeed without any real understanding of what Upperton (Heaven) calls success.

Calvin Miller in *The Valiant Papers*

TIME OUT
By Shirley Giles Davis

Shirley Giles Davis graduated from Stanford University with a degree in communications broadcasting and studied economics and political science at Stanford in Tours, France. Since then she has worked as a radio broadcaster, producer, and fundraiser. In addition to sustaining a busy career, Shirley is on the executive committee for the Professional Women's Fellowship, and she and her husband, Rob, a professor in chemical engineering at the University of Colorado, are the lay directors for the University Christian Fellowship in Boulder. How she manages her tightly packed schedule? She says . . .

As I began to think about writing some helpful hints on time management, I came to realize that I seem to learn the most about effective time management when I am not doing it very well. There are five questions that I have begun to ask myself whenever I feel I am ineffectively spinning too many plates. Those questions are:

1. Question of control: Am I in control of my situation, or do I let my situation control me?

2. Question of priorities: Do I let the urgent shut out the important?

3. Question of commitments: Do I over-commit such that time management is a ridiculous proposition?

4. What/who is my first priority and how can I tell? (A good way to find this out is to look at checkbook stubs and appointment book.)

5. Am I investing a good proportion of my time in something eternal (involving people) or in something temporal?

I have found that effective time management requires regular reassessment and a need for flexibility balanced with self-protection. By this I mean that to be more effective in the other demands of life and work, one needs to schedule some time for oneself to regroup and quietly await God's leading.

6

GOING FOR THE GOLD

A clear definition of goals is the keynote of success.

Edison Montgomery

Normally I'm not what you would call a football fan, except for the week when Colorado's pro team, the Denver Broncos, won the AFC Championship and a trip to the Super Bowl. So, big deal. If you've seen one AFC Championship you've seen them all. Right? Well, not necessarily. Even for us not-so-interested, *very* fair-weather fans, it was a game to remember. Until the final minutes of the game, the Broncos were tied with the Cleveland Browns 13–13. Then the Browns made a touchdown and the extra point, placing the Ohio team in a 20–13 lead. Everyone—the coaches, the fans, the media—pretty much knew that the Broncos had lost. It was time to go home. Right?

Wrong again. With the clock ticking through the last two

minutes of the game, and the Browns fans smug with victory, Denver's star quarterback John Elway moved his team a miraculous 98 yards from the Broncos' own 2-yard line to make a touchdown that, with the added help of the extra point, pushed the game into a tiebreaker. As the Broncos positioned themselves for the tiebreaking kick, thousands of fans in the stands and thousands more from their living rooms held their breath. Executed by a nervous and barefooted Rich Karlis, the kick was somewhat off-center but passed poetically between the goalposts, giving the Broncos a three-point advantage, the game, and the veneration of those who watched.

Talk about Broncomania! "98 Yards to Glory" read the next morning's headlines. It was the talk of the town, and beyond the normal boundaries of vicariousness, a pervasive "We're Winners!" mentality blanketed the state.

So why am I telling a primarily female readership about a football game? Because John Elway's come-from-behind, refusal-to-lose, let's-go-for-the-gold chutzpah is not for men only. It's for us, too. As Christians, we are called to come from behind despite the odds against us and lay claim to the victory that is already ours. We are called to run in such a way that we win (1 Cor. 9:24).

But if we want to win, we must *plan* to win. One of the things that helped the Broncos win was that they had set the *goal* to win and that they had *trained* to win. The fact is, they had achieved numerous "wins," they had reached numerous smaller goals on the practice field and throughout the season that enabled them to "go for the gold" on that memorable winter afternoon. And so it must be for us.

Winners don't set limits, they set goals.

Author Unknown

1. Read the following verses and note how they relate to having an athletic Christian experience. Next to each verse, write the character quality that contributes to a spiritual "win."

1 Corinthians 9:25 *Self discipline*

Hebrews 12:1 *Patience*

1 John 5:4 *Faith*

1 Timothy 4:7–8 *Promise Godliness*

Philippians 3:13–14 *Forgetting past & press forward*

2. Read Philippians 3:7–12 and list the apostle Paul's personal goals.

Win for Christ, evaluating things.
Setting priorities, Know Christ

Whether you think you can or think you can't, you're right.

Henry Ford

3. As part of an exercise to think through and establish your own personal goals, purchase a stack of 3 x 5 index cards.

a. On one of the cards, write "Lifetime Goals" at the top. On this card, write your major life objectives, what you want to achieve broadly. (In doing this exercise, you may need to use several 3 x 5 cards to list all the goals in a particular category.) My own "Lifetime Goals" include such general statements as, "knowing Christ," "loving others," "making a significant contribution through my abilities." These may seem vague at first, but many times they have been pivotal to major decisions I have had to make. For example, soon after I did this exercise for the first time, I was asked to join a professional music group that would tour the West Coast. Initially it sounded like a rather attractive opportunity (I'm not sure why—nor why I was asked; my musical interests and abilities are marginal at best), but in reviewing my "Lifetime Goals," I was reminded that being a part of this group clearly was not going in keeping with my long-term goals. Over the long haul, it was a tangent. I'm still glad I turned down the opportunity; it freed my time for endeavors that made better use of my abilities.

b. On another card, write "Five-Year Goals." On this card write down the things you would like to accomplish during the next five years in the following categories, keeping your "Lifetime Goals" in mind.

Spiritual goals	*Financial goals*
Mental goals	*Social goals*
Professional goals	*Physical goals*

Be somewhat specific and be honest with yourself. Don't try to spiritualize everything you hope to accomplish. Wanting to get an MBA so you can get a higher salary is a perfectly legitimate desire if you have filtered it through God's hands in prayer. If it's not the direction the Lord wants you to take, He'll show you. But as long as you *want* to do it, it is worthy of your every consideration.

c. Then on the back of the 3 x 5 cards that contain your "Five-Year Goals," answer the following questions for each goal:

Why do I want to accomplish this goal?
What steps must I take to accomplish it?

What would prevent me from accomplishing it?
What must I do to overcome these obstacles?

d. On the next set of 3 x 5 cards, write at the top, "One-Year Goals." List the same categories as before, but get more specific. For example, if one of your "Five-Year Goals" is visiting Paris, write down how much money you need to set aside this year, when you need to start French lessons, etc. You also will want to include miscellaneous short-term goals on this set of cards that may or may not have any relation to your "Five-Year Goals." For example, you might want to clean out your files. While it may not have cosmic or cascading implications, it is still something you need to do and thus merits a spot on the card. Plan to update your "One-Year Goals" every January and to review your "One-Year Goals" at the beginning of each month, marking off the items you have accomplished and scheduling in the items you need to work on during the month that follows. As the year progresses, you may periodically need to adjust a goal to be more realistic or more in keeping with new insights and experiences.

e. On the back of the cards that contain your "One-Year Goals," once again answer these questions, perhaps more briefly than before.

Why do I want to accomplish this goal?
What steps must I take to accomplish it?
What would prevent me from accomplishing it?
What must I do to overcome these obstacles?

The first time you do this exercise will probably take a considerably larger amount of time and thought than it will in subsequent years—but it's worth the initial investment.

I keep my written goals in a 15" file box designed for 3 x 5 cards (available at office supply stores) under a section I have simply entitled "Goals." I also have marked off sections entitled: Quotes, Jokes, Stories, Ideas & Insights, and Miscellaneous. Whenever I read a book, I use a 3 x 5 card as my bookmark. On the top of the card, I write down the book title, the author, publisher, and copyright date. As I read along, I write down notable quotes and include the page number where I found it. Most of the quotes I have included in this workshop are from the "Quote" section of my box. As a writer, I have found this to be an invaluable resource. I also turn to this section when I need a bit of encouragement or inspiration. Of course, in establishing a file, you will want to section it off according to your own professional and personal interests.

The journey of a thousand miles begins with a single step.

Chinese Proverb

TIME OUT
By Mary Anne Lausterer

Mary Anne is a practicing X-ray technician and is currently completing training as an emergency medical technician. She also is a licensed real estate saleswoman and is the mother of four children. Her flaming auburn hair is characteristic of the fire and originality with which she approaches her life—and her time. When faced with a unique time management problem, she developed and implemented a unique and workable solution. Says she . . .

SCENARIO I: The setting is a small town in upstate New York on a cold and drizzly February evening. I'm driving home from a day of work at a family medical practice where I am the office nurse and technician. The windshield wipers on my station wagon flip/flop before my eyes as I listen to my two young sons in the back seat and contemplate what I am going to fix for dinner. Why didn't I remember to take the roast out of the freezer before I left that morning? (These were "B.M.O." days—before microwave ovens.)

As we approached our home, I am annoyed by the darkness surrounding the house—we lived in the country then; and stumbling through the dark, I remove the boys, their gear and mine, and head for the house. Good grief! There's my newspaper in the wet, sloppy snow. Yuk! Once inside the house, we are greeted by an older brother and sister who have just arrived from the neighbors, and by K.C. (Kids Canine), the family dog who is jumping all over me begging me to feed her. During the next several hours I prepare, serve and clean up after the evening meal; bathe and prepare four small children for bed; change the baby at least three times; put two loads of laundry through the washer and dryer; fold diapers; sweep the kitchen floor; pick up the toy room (it's a proven fact that children will NOT play in a messy room), and finally collapse in my chair with a crinkled, soggy newspaper. Some time later I fall into bed, exhausted.

SCENARIO II: Several months later, the time and setting are the same. As the two small boys and I alight from our car, the glow from our driveway and porch lamps light our way into the house. I can smell dinner cooking in the oven that was put on automatic "start" before I left in the morning. The newspaper has been carefully placed on the stand next to my favorite reading chair. Over in the corner lies a sleeping K.C., having just finished her dinner, and there is fresh water in her dish. The kitchen table is properly set and ready for me to serve dinner. The lunch boxes are emptied, rinsed, and stacked on the counter and the dryer is whirring softly as the diapers tumble around in it. When I go up to my bedroom to change clothes, I see my pile of folded laundry sitting neatly on the bed waiting for me to place it in my dresser drawers.

After dinner the table is cleared by two of the children; the room is straightened up by two others. One child has folded the now-dry diapers and has placed them in their space on the changing table. K.C. has been let out and back in when necessary and I've hardly noticed. A while later I am hearing prayers from small mouths and snuggling precious bodies into beds. A few minutes with a cup of herb tea and the evening newspaper and I am renewed to complete my evening's activities. I'm going to bed earlier . . . to sleep and REST.

What, you may ask, made the difference in these scenarios? Some have said that life has not been the same since man invented the wheel, and certainly that has been the case since the invention of the "work wheel." This is a simple idea I gleaned from a women's magazine and promptly put to use.

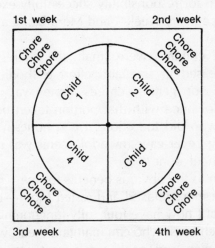

The basic design is to take a piece of rectangularly shaped cardboard and mount on top of it a circular piece of cardboard attached with a small gold paperfastener. In our case, the circular cardboard was divided into four sections, each with a child's name printed in it, along with the numbers 1 through 4. Section #1 also had a red dot on it, to determine where to begin. The rectangular cardboard had various household and family chores written in each of the four corners, and each corner was marked as the first through the fourth weeks in the month. At the beginning of each month, the red dot was turned to correspond with week #1 on the rectangle. The child named in that section was responsible for the corresponding chores for one week, and so forth around the circle with other names and chores. Each Sunday, I turned the wheel and each child then was responsible for the next set of chores that now corresponded with his/her name. Naturally, four children and four weeks per month made this quite simple.

The reward for responsibility successfully executed was a full allowance every week—and Mom being a nicer person to be around.

When the children were small, the chores were small. Chores increased in size and effort as bodies grew. The penalty for not getting chores done was a decreased collected allowance with that portion taken being given to the person who did the chore. I can honestly say that the most nagging I ever gave my adolescents was my query, "Is the work wheel done?"

In addition to the obvious benefits for me—more time for myself and a more relaxed and rested Mom—the long-term benefit is that I now have four fully-functioning college and high school children who can maintain their own rooms and belongings, plan and cook meals, sort and wash clothes without ruining them (and three of them are boys!).

Recently, thanks to the author of this book, I have

redesigned a work wheel to use in my own life and activities as a mother, friend, employed professional, and student. Life goes on . . . as the wheel turns.

Part III

TIME KILLERS

7

PRIDE AND PREJUDICE

Pride gets no pleasure out of having something, only out of having more of it than the next man.

C.S. Lewis

At Christmastime I marveled at my six-year-old niece. Despite the pile of presents she had received, all of them carefully selected with her kindergarten wants and needs in mind, she longingly looked over at the holiday accumulation of her two-year-old brother, who was delighting in one present in particular—a flashlight that he was repeatedly turning on and off and mischievously pointing in the eyes of his aunts and uncles (who weren't annoyed, because he was so cute). Watching this scenario, my niece moved to a corner, her unhappiness becoming apparent as our present opening ritual proceeded. We soon learned the source of her sorrow—her brother had gotten a flashlight and she hadn't.

Not that she particularly wanted a flashlight. It was just that, well, you know, he had one and she didn't. It didn't seem to matter that she had received many things that her brother had not.

Unfortunately, it is a long-term and readily contagious disease. We travel through adolescence wanting the outfit someone else has, their boyfriend, or their popularity; through college wanting another's scholastic achievement, svelte figure, their car; and into adulthood, no longer wanting what everyone else has—the fact is that we want *more*. Because of envy maturing into pride, we spend countless hours and dollars so that our neighbors will admire us—and the ultimate compliment—emulate us.

But to sustain the aura of superiority that we somehow think will win us admiration and opportunity, we learn that we cannot associate with certain people—people whose educational background, bank account, or social standing does not affirm or in some way contribute to our climb to the stars. We do not call it pride and prejudice, of course. That's too harsh. Rather we call it "a sense of excellence," or "good taste."

Unfortunately, cultivating our pride, which in turn cultivates our prejudices, is a subtle and time-consuming enterprise which erodes our productivity, our focus, and our sense of priority. For all the efforts we expend to convince ourselves and others that we are better than they are, rarely does it return to us the genuine esteem we are seeking.

How does pride and prejudice affect our time and our lives? How can we effectively and repeatedly lay it aside for more productive endeavors? These are questions that will be briefly explored in this lesson.

1. In John 4:4–42 we learn about a circumstance in which Jesus ignored some rather well-established social norms. Read these verses, noting the following:

a. He traveled through Samaria, an area the Jews of His day typically circumvented in honor of a well-worn prejudice.

b. He spoke with a woman in public, not done under any circumstances and especially not (as was the case here) with a woman whose sexual practices hardly placed her in the "nice-girl-next-door" category.

2. Why do you think Jesus ignored these social dictates? *To be a example to his decyples - to train them.*

3. How did He treat the woman at the well, who by all normal standards was "beneath" Him? *He treated her well - He knew her inward ways.*

> *No person is strong enough to carry a cross and a prejudice at the same time.*
>
> William A. Ward

4. What are some accepted social practices in our culture that clearly are not in keeping with Christianity? _____

_____

_____

5. How do these prejudices affect the way we manage our time? How is our time different when we lay them aside? ___

_____

_____

6. Read James 2:1–10. What does James (Jesus' younger brother) admonish us not to do? *Not to show favoritism. Love our neighbor as our self.*

_____

_____

*A man must not choose his neighbor; he must take the
neighbor that God sends him.*

George MacDonald

7. What are some of the common sources of pride in our
culture? It it wrong to accomplish or possess these things? At
what point do they become a source of pride?

8. What was Paul's attitude toward his accomplishments
and possessions, according to Philippians 3:4–8? _____

_____

_____

9. And Philippians 4:11–14? *Contentment
with his circumstances*

_____

10. Read the following verses and summarize what each
has to say about pride—and humility.

Psalm 10:4	Jeremiah 49:16
Proverbs 11:2	1 John 2:16–17
Proverbs 16:18–19	James 4:6

*Benefits of being humble — Sobrew
happiness.*

_____

_____

*But it is not the rich man only who is under the dominion
of things; they too are slaves who, having no money, are
unhappy from the lack of it.*

George MacDonald

11. Are there any ways you feel that God would have you spend your time, but your pride and/or prejudices are keeping you from carrying it out—at least carrying it out with enthusiasm? How are you spending the time you should be allotting to this? _____

_____

_____

12. Read 1 Peter 5:5 and discuss what you think it means to "clothe yourselves with humility." _____

Humble to admit you can learn from one another.

13. Conclude by reading Psalm 131.

In Christian service, the branches that bear the most fruit hang the lowest.

Author Unknown

TIME OUT
By Diana Juhlin

Diana is a corporate manager—big on brains and small on words, and somewhat of an efficiency expert. She juggles her demanding job (that sometimes requires her to travel) with her marriage to husband Bruce (a computer analyst for AT&T), her responsibilities as mother to toddler Briana, and her ministry with high school students. Of time management, she says . . .

Some things should be handled immediately so as not to waste time handling them over and over again. One item that fits into this category is mail. If you throw, file, or process your mail when you open it, rather than sticking it in a pile, then you will have to handle it only once. Many other small repetitive tasks should be handled in this manner.

8

DISOBEDIENCE

We have the tragic, mistaken idea that we must choose between doing what we want and being happy, and doing what God wants us to do and being miserable. Nothing could be further from the truth.

Paul Little

Sandwiched in between two other minor prophets in the Old Testament, we find a short but insightful missive about a man named Jonah, whom God called into His service. "Arise, go to Nineveh the great city, and cry against it, for their wickedness has come up before Me," God commissioned him (Jonah 1:2, NASB). Unflattered that God deemed him worthy of the task and obviously unwilling to carry it out for reasons not clearly stated in the text, Jonah disobeys God, and as the story goes, he "rose up to flee to Tarshish from the presence of the Lord" (Jonah 1:3).

Hardly the model for spiritual maturity. But part of us

understands how Jonah must have felt: "You don't understand, God, I don't *want* to walk the cold, lonely streets of Nineveh telling those nice folks what a bunch of sinners they are. It's just not going to win me any popularity contests. So go do your own dirty work. And hey, in the future don't call me, I'll call you." The next thing we know, Jonah has boarded a ship sailing upstream against the will of God.

But through a most unusual series of circumstances, Jonah changes his mind, if not his heart, and in Jonah 3:1 we read, "Now the word of the Lord came to Jonah the second time, saying 'Arise, go to Nineveh the great city and proclaim to it the proclamation which I am going to tell you.' So Jonah arose and went to Nineveh according to the word of the Lord."

Somehow between God's first call and His second, Jonah found reason to be obedient. I suspect that three days in the belly of a whale gave him time to reconsider. As it turns out, God used Jonah to salvage the spiritual vitality of an entire city. Ultimately, God's will was done. Jonah would have saved a lot of time, however, had he obeyed God the first time around—and so would we. Our disobedience only delays the blessings God wants to give us and other people *through* us. Somehow we have developed the notion that God (who we imagine to be inexplicably and incessantly angry with us) is out to get us if we don't wholeheartedly obey His (unreasonable) demands, and that at the first opportunity He has, He will toss us overboard to be swallowed by some proverbial giant fish. He did it to Jonah, therefore what would keep Him from doing it to us, we speculate. But we fail to recognize that the fish did not hurt Jonah; the fact is, it saved him from the fatal elements of the sea. As was the case with Jonah, God works with us to give us a second chance for a blessing.

1. Read these verses and summarize what they have to say about obedience.

> 1 Peter 1:22   Hebrews 5:8–9
> Acts 5:29
> Romans 5:19

purified the soul – obedience to God
Obedience brings righteousness – Through
suffering

2. Then read Romans 5:19, and discuss how our obedience affects not only our own lives, but the lives of others as well. How does our disobedience affect others? *It effects*
others because the use that we
excuse friends

3. In Genesis 22:1–10, we read about Abraham, on whom God placed a most difficult test of obedience. Do you think Abraham wanted to slay his son? Why do you think he obeyed God anyway, despite some conflicting emotions he may have had? *He had faith in God*
to either bring his son back or provide
a substitute.

> *Spiritual maturity comes not by erudition, but by compliance with the known will of God.*
>
> Leonard Ravenhill

4. What was the result of Abraham's obedience, according to Genesis 22:11–14? Why do you think God tested Abraham in this manner? What do you think would have happened if Abraham had not obeyed God? And what do you think were the reciprocating, long-term effects of Abraham's obedience in his own life, in the life of his son, and in the lives of God's people? _____

_____

_____

5. Has there been an occasion when you felt God asked you to obey Him in a matter that at first seemed as if He did not have your best interests in mind? Did you obey or disobey Him? What were the immediate and reciprocating results? _____

_____

_____

> . . . *even the very wise cannot see all ends.*
>
> J.R.R. Tolkien in *Fellowship of the Ring*

6. Read Matthew 9:10–13 and discuss what you think Jesus meant and how it relates to obedience—and to time management. _____

_____

_____

7. According to Hebrews 11:8–10, what seems to be a prerequisite to obedience? _____

_____

_____

8. Why was Sarah, Abraham's wife, able to be obedient according to Hebrews 11:11? _____

_____

_____

9. Read Philippians 2:12–18 and list all the things the apostle Paul admonishes us to do to cultivate our obedience to God. _____

---

10. Conclude by reading Psalm 143:10–12. _____

Faith never knows where it is being led, but it loves and knows the One who is leading.

Oswald Chambers

TIME OUT
By Maggie Lee

An accomplished musician and songwriter, the sole proprietor of a bookkeeping business, the mother of two boys and wife to husband Dave, an architect, Maggie faces an unusually diverse set of demands on her time and interests. How does she effectively manage her time when she can, and what does she do when she can't? She says ...

Time management is a wonderful concept on paper, but it is not always easy to put into practical use. Because I run a part-time business out of my home while raising two young children, there are two important ingredients I add to my concept of time management.

The first ingredient is *discipline with flexibility*. I plan my weekly agenda and brace myself for the week to come. Invariably something comes up to interrupt these plans, such as chicken pox or the highly contagious and universally dreaded disease known by all mothers as "pink eye." I find that being disciplined enough to plan my week is good, but flexibility is paramount to my sanity.

The second equally important ingredient is *a sense of humor.* Something as simple as planning my weekly schedule seems quite easy, but my plans are often interrupted, and I find myself getting upset by these "serious" setbacks to my well-ordered agenda. My sense of humor has seen me through many a week, such as when all my plans were tossed aside with the simple phrase: "Mrs. Lee, your child has pneumonia and needs bed rest and *no outings* for a week." Oh yes, a sense of humor is a must.

The discipline of planning my time organizes my priorities for each week. Whether or not my schedule is followed, I believe that the exercise of planning my time makes me more effective in managing the various aspects of my life.

9

ANXIETY

One of the drawbacks about adventures is that when you come to the most beautiful places you are often too anxious and hurried to appreciate them.

C.S. Lewis

Somewhere along the line—I'm not exactly sure when—I decided that I wanted to spend my first few years out of college doing some things that were wildly adventuresome— some things I suspected I would not have the energy or idealism to do later on. One of the outcomes of this decision was that I became involved with an organization that sends medical, teaching, and engineering teams to developing nations. It seemed to fit the bill for the adventure I was seeking.

As adventure and circumstance (and God) would have it, I soon found myself in Iloilo, a city in central Philippines, where I was assigned to teach for the summer as a guest lecturer at Central Philippines University. I lived with the family of the dean of students, enjoying their company and learning from them how to eat, sleep, and think like a Filipino. In between my duties and their hospitality, I easily found time to take a language class, tutor some gymnastics, go on a jeep and canoe trip, and visit the neighboring islands—it was at once a challenging and restful summer.

But for all the rich experiences my summer in Iloilo provided, the slow steamy life of the Southeast Pacific grated against my Type A personality. I had no pressing deadlines— I love deadlines; no high pressure demands—I thrive on pressure; and no skintight schedules to shorten my lifespan. By the end of the summer I was eager to get back to the frantic, befrazzled society that I call home.

Thus, at summer's end, bags packed and more than ready to go, I left for Manila to rejoin my American colleagues who had been assigned to other Asian sites. We went to the airport together, chattering, and perhaps at times exaggerating, about our separate experiences. But when it was my turn at the airport counter, the ticket agent dutifully informed me as he flipped through my ticket jacket of used stubs that I did not have a return ticket to the U.S. and therefore could not board the airplane.

"But that can't be," I replied in the most genuine and embarrassed of terms. "I purchased the ticket myself—it *must* be there. Another agent must have accidently torn it off in San Francisco or Guam during one of my incoming stopovers," I explained, knowing I did not have the money to purchase another $900 ticket. I felt my anxiety level rise when he returned a blank stare. It was obvious that no amount of persuasion on my part was going to inspire him to let me board the plane. My anxiety level rose still more as several members of my party got involved and in turn explained to him that I was with them, we had all come to

the Philippines together, and asked if he could overlook this
one minor detail just this once.

"No deal," he said emphatically. "The woman has no
ticket and therefore she cannot board the airplane."

At that point I lost my sense of humor and my reason, and
visions of being stuck forever and ever in that hot little
country with no money and only one suitcase and 1/4 bottle
of my favorite shampoo raced across my renegade imagination. How would I employ myself? Where would I live? How
would I survive malaria when my pasty little pills ran out?
(etcetera), were questions I irrationally and prematurely tried
to answer. At least one thing was certain—I would not be
leaving the Philippines—at least not that night.

The people who had brought my team members to the
airport graciously offered to put me up for the night and help
me work it out in the morning, so we put my suitcase in their
car and headed back to their home. In spite of my
frustrations, as we traveled through the dark streets of Manila,
I could feel the presence of God.

I wish I could tell you that I matched His gentle invasion
into my circumstances with an investment of faith—but I did
not. Moments later, muttering under my breath, I sent up
steaming thoughts of disappointment and discomfort:
"Would You mind getting me out of this mess—and why did
You put me in it in the first place!"

Despite my less-than-noble response, God was faithful (a
rather nice habit of His). As we drove up in front of the
driver's house—by then it was 1:30 a.m.—her husband
came running into the street in his pajamas, and leaning in
the window, he said breathlessly: "One of guys called the
president of Philippine Airlines and got him out of bed—he
told him everything. The president has ordered the airport to
let you on the plane. So turn around and hurry back—they're

holding the flight for you." I couldn't believe it! Sheepishly I muttered an apology to God.

By the time I got back to the airport, my story had circulated so that when I walked into the airport terminal, the two hundred or so people who were sitting in the waiting area offered me a standing ovation, glad to see the little guy win out.

All of that anxiety for naught. But then, anxiety always is. It's not that I wasted *more* time because I was anxious, it was just that I wasted the precious time that was meant for something else. I learned an important lesson from that experience, and have never been anxious since (well, maybe just a few times since then).

1. According to the dictionary, what is anxiety? _____

_____

_____

2. Read the following verses and write down what each verse tells us to do about anxiety.

   Matthew 6:34   Philippians 4:6
   Luke 12:24–26

_____

_____

_____

3. What should we do when we are anxious, according to 1 Peter 5:7? _____

_____

_____

> *Ulcers are something you get from mountain-climbing over molehills.*
>
>   Author Unknown

4. In Acts 16:22–24, we learn that Paul and his co-worker, Silas, were beaten and thrown into jail—understandably anxiety-producing circumstances for anyone. Read Acts 16:25 and summarize how Paul and Silas responded to their adverse circumstances. _____

_____

_____

5. Then read Acts 16:26–30 and describe in your own words what happened next, noting in particular God's faithfulness. _____

_____

_____

6. Similarly in Daniel 3:13–23, we learn that Daniel's friends were thrown into a furnace, again an understandable reason for anxiety. What was the outcome of their circumstances, according to Daniel 3:24–27? _____

_____

_____

Anxiety does not empty tomorrow of its sorrows, but only empties today of its strength.

Charles Spurgeon

7. How can we build our faith, as suggested by these verses, and thus become less prone to anxiety?

Romans 10:17   *1 Thessalonians 5:16–18*
Hebrews 12:1–2

_____

_____

8. Take five 3 x 5 cards and on each card write down one circumstance in which you felt anxious. Then for each circumstance, write down a response to the following questions.

a. What was the source of your anxiety?

b. How was God faithful in remedying the situation?

c. What verses, books, or people did God use to help you or guide you during this time? Summarize what was helpful.

d. What did you learn from this experience?

e. How would you like to respond differently the next time you are anxious?

When you have completed the questions, make a section in the file established earlier in this workshop entitled "Remembrances" and put the cards in it. Then turn to this section when you become anxious in the future to remind yourself of God's faithfulness. Also, add to it whenever another situation gets resolved.

9. Conclude by reading Isaiah 41:10.

> *But the Christian . . . knows that he not only cannot and dare not be anxious, but that there is also no need for him to be so.*
>
> Dietrich Bonhoeffer

TIME OUT
By Sara Randall

Sara and her husband, Roger, are international representatives for Campus Crusade for Christ, which takes them on the road nationally and internationally throughout the year. Thriving on a nonstop schedule, Sara frequently speaks to college students and professional women, and she has been named "A Woman Who Makes a Difference" by *Today's Christian Woman* magazine. She also is co-founder of the Professional Women's Fellowship of Boulder and is mother to eight-year-old Allison.

My favorite time management help is the KISS method— "Keep it simple, stupid." I can't control much of life, but what I can, I simplify. Some "keep it simple" tips:

1. Keep *one* calendar, one address book, one shopping list, one "To Do" list, etc. Keep them together in *one* notebook.

Mine goes everywhere with me and sits on my desk when I'm at home.

2. Keep a plastic ziplock baggie in your purse containing your basic small needs. In my baggie is lipstick, powder, nail file, nail polish, hand cream, breath spray, aspirin, kleenex, travel packets of wash and dries, and a pen. When I need to change purses, I grab the baggie and switch.

3. Don't laugh, but I use only one color of lipstick that goes well with my coloring and my clothes. In addition to the lipstick in my baggie, I keep one in my makeup bag and one in the bathroom drawer, so that I don't have to search for it when I need it. In fact, I have an extra of all my basic makeup in the bathroom drawer. For those who travel as I do, it's helpful to keep a small makeup bag with travel sizes of everything packed and ready to go. I can take it to the YMCA to swim or to Africa for a month. If you wear glasses that you put on and take off frequently, it's helpful to buy several pair. Keep one in your purse, one by the bed, and one on your desk.

4. Plan the next day the night before. Load the car the night before with the items you will be toting the next day— Susie's guitar for her lesson, dry cleaning, library books, briefcases, etc. Also have the kids choose their own clothes the night before. Do the same for yourself. (Let your husband attend to his own preparations in this respect.) Also, go to bed 15 minutes earlier than usual, and have everyone in the family get up 15 minutes earlier than usual—it really makes a difference.

CONCLUSION:
BEYOND THE TIME BARRIER

The created world is but a small parenthesis in eternity.

Sir Thomas Browne

Of all the mysteries of the cosmos, perhaps the most fascinating and frightening to us is the mystery that awaits us on the other side of time, in eternity—in time without time.

Trying to anticipate the infinite with finite, cowardly imaginations is near to impossible, and we are prone to be anemic at best, but more often errant and unfounded conclusions as to what it will be like. One current, widely marketed notion tells us that eternity is a succession of reincarnated lives; thus we pop in and out of time and space like biological yo-yos, never really getting to enjoy the peace and promise of heaven, for heaven is no more than a split-second stopover between karmas. Gary Trudeau, the caustic creator of *Doonesbury*, recently poked fun at this theology in his daily strip, portraying his vain, gullible Boopsie worrying about sun-damaged skin in a past life when she is urged to bow down and worship the Egyptian sun god, Ra.

We laugh at this, but "Christian" concepts of heaven and eternity often are based on equally ridiculous theological ground. One concept has us sitting on a cloud strumming a harp with an ethereal, faraway look on our faces; another has us forever chained to the throne of God repeating incessantly, "Holy, holy, holy." Given even a moment of consideration, one can hardly find such an existence appealing.

The fact is, for the most part we do not know what awaits us. We do, however, know *Who* awaits us—and we know from the brief glimpses of heaven that our Lord gives us that we have much to look forward to. When studied, His glimpses lend much understanding and perspective to the time that we now have the extraordinary opportunity to manage.

1. In John 17:3, Jesus defines eternal life. Read what He has to say and capsulize His thoughts in your own words.____

_____

_____

2. Given Jesus' definition, when do you think we step inside eternity? _____

_____

_____

3. Similarly, when do you think we begin enjoying heaven, according to John the Baptist in Matthew 3:2?_____

_____

_____

Eternal life is not a gift from God, eternal life is the gift of God.

Oswald Chambers

4. In Matthew 13, Jesus draws for us some mental sketches of life beyond the time barrier. Read verses 24–50 [or 47] and summarize what they tell us about "the kingdom of heaven."

(Matthew 13:24–30; 13:36–43)

Matthew 13:31–43   Matthew 13:45–46
Matthew 13:33   Matthew 13:47
Matthew 13:44

_____

_____

5. The verses noted above intimate that the evil counterfeit of creation—Satan's attempt to be like God—will be dealt with in final terms, and that entrance into the kingdom of heaven is a costly enterprise. What price was paid so that God's war against sin would be won so that we could become citizens of eternity, according to John 3:16?_____

_____

_____

6. What was God's objective in ransoming His Son on our behalf, according to John 3:17?_____

_____

_____

7. Read the following verses and note next to each one what awaits us beyond the time barrier.

John 14:2 _____

Revelation 21:3–5 _____

1 Corinthians 13:12 _____

1 Corinthians 2:9 _____

Joy is the serious business of heaven.

C.S. Lewis

8. Death, then, is not the cessation of life, but rather, for the Christian, a doorway into nearer union with our Creator. What do these verses say to us about death?

John 8:51 _____

Psalm 48:14 _____

1 John 3:14 _____

Psalm 116:15 _____

9. Read Philippians 1:20–21 and summarize the apostle Paul's attitude toward death.

_____

_____

10. As a final exercise in this workshop, consider how you might spend your time differently if you knew when you were going to die. Our days on this side of time are, in fact, numbered. List three things you would like to work on in particular in the months ahead that will enable you to give your time and your life more completely and more cheerfully to the Lord, who created time for our benefit so that we might know a little bit more of:

His splendor _____

His order _____

His reason _____

His imagination _____

His boundless love _____

Let us live as people who are prepared to die, and die as people who are prepared to live.

James S. Stewart